FUNDAMENTALS OF TENNIS

Stanley Plagenhoef

FUNDAMENTALS OF TENNIS

PRENTICE-HALL, INC., Englewood Cliffs, New Jersey

© 1970 by Prentice-Hall, Inc., Englewood Cliffs, New Jersey

13-344606-9

Library of Congress Catalog Card Number: 77-101530

Printed in the United States of America

Current Printing (Last Digit)

10 9 8 7 6 5 4 3 2 1

PRENTICE-HALL INTERNATIONAL, Inc., *London*
PRENTICE-HALL OF AUSTRALIA, PTY. LTD., *Sydney*
PRENTICE-HALL OF CANADA, LTD., *Toronto*
PRENTICE-HALL OF INDIA PRIVATE LTD., *New Delhi*
PRENTICE-HALL OF JAPAN, INC., *Tokyo*

'72

71

To the Youth Development Program of Holland, Michigan,
to my coaches, Joe Moran and L. M. Williams,
and to my hundreds of pupils at Prouts Neck, Maine,
Fairfield Beach Club, Connecticut,
Bath and Tennis Club, Spring Lake, New Jersey,
and Wesleyan University

Illustrated by

NELSON GILES

Contributing Artists

DON CURTIS
ROBINY CASE
JUDY PIHL

Tracing reductions

LOUIS MUSANTE

Contents

Introduction

All of the illustrations in FUNDAMENTALS OF TENNIS are drawings made from selected frames of motion pictures, those that
best illustrate the mechanics involved in hitting a tennis ball.
Many times a specific subject was used because the pictures obtained were precisely correct to illustrate a certain point, and not
because this person was unique in performing a certain skill.

Views from directly behind or in front of a player or at a right
angle to the ball flight were needed to properly show the strokes
and individual differences. These exact angles were often difficult
to obtain at ground level during tournament play. I thank the
many players who could hear the film buzzing through the
camera at 64 frames per second, but did not request silence. In
addition to slow motion, the camera was set at 1/4 open shutter
for each frame to have an exposure of 1/512 second. This is
adequate to stop the racket head and ball even during the serve
so that accurate individual drawings could be made.

A combined background of teaching tennis to pupils of all
ages, of both sexes, with a wide range of ability, and teaching
anatomy and kinesiology led to this presentation, mixing factual
data with experience. I hope beginners, advanced players, and
teachers may find something that will help them improve upon
skills and provide more hours of enjoyable play.

Stanley Plagenhoef

FUNDAMENTALS OF TENNIS

chapter 1

GRIPS

The firmness of the grip at impact is the single most important factor in hitting a tennis ball. A player strives to be in the most advantageous position at impact, which means consideration of bone structure, muscular strength, and rhythm and timing of the swing. The grip will determine the point of contact in relation to the body. A grip cannot be correct unless the point of contact is also known. The further the hand is moved toward the back of the racket, on either the forehand or backhand, the further forward must be the contact point for straight shots.

FOREHAND GRIPS

The Eastern forehand is probably the most universally taught forehand grip because it facilitates hitting balls at all heights with equal ease (Figure 1–1a). The hand is behind the racket and if the hand were opened, the palm would be perpendicular to the ground (Figure 1–1b). The base knuckle of the thumb is centered on top. A few beginners prefer an extreme back position, a grip I discourage (Figure 1–2). Any player who persists with this grip has difficulty with low balls or tends to play deeper in the court; this tendency results in a looping forehand with a dropped racket head. This benefits the opponent by giving him more time for

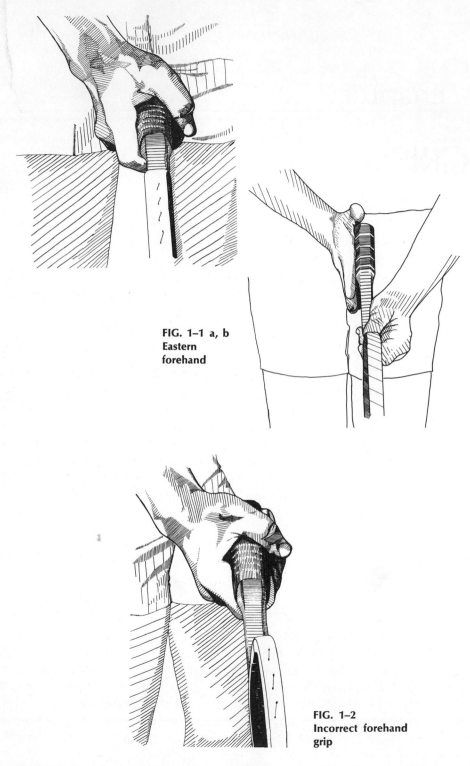

FIG. 1–1 a, b
Eastern
forehand

FIG. 1–2
Incorrect forehand
grip

recovery off the previous shot. The point of contact for the Eastern grip is between the center of the body and the left heel, with slight variations owing to individual differences. Check three points when the racket is placed at the contact point: 1) the placement of the palm behind the handle, 2) the spread of the fingers, and 3) the butt end just out of the hand. If all of these points are correct, the wrist should be in its strongest position. Spreading of the fingers is necessary to keep the wrist in a strong position when reaching for the ball; if the fingers are not spread, there is undue stress on the thumb side of the wrist with a weakening of the grip. Playing with the butt end up in the hand also results in a weakened grip.

The Continental grip places the hand toward the top of the racket with the V of the thumb and finger on top (Figure 1–3a). This grip is best suited for low balls, and it also causes a player to slice balls at a lower height than the Eastern grip. If the hand were opened, the palm would be angled toward the ground (Figure 1–3b). The point of contact must be about at the center of the body to keep the wrist in a strong position. This grip is most suited to grass court play, in which the approach and volley dominate the game, resulting in a high proportion of low shots.

FIG. 1–3 a, b
Continental grip

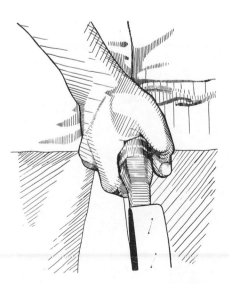
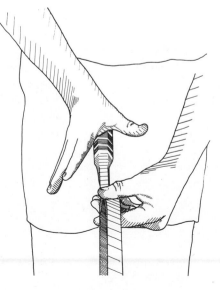

Many players use the Continental grip for the backhand, but the Eastern backhand is better for play on surfaces other than grass. With the Eastern backhand the base knuckle of the index finger is rotated on top of the handle with the thumb placed *diagonally* across the back. The tip of the thumb will then be between the first and second fingers (Figure 1–4 a, b). If the hand is opened, the palm is approximately parallel to the ground (Figure 1–4c). With the fingers spread and the butt end just out

**FIG. 1–4 a, b, c
Eastern backhand grip**

FIG. 1–5 a, b
Incorrect, thumb up, backhand grip

of the hand, the point of contact must be forward of the right foot to retain a straight wrist at contact. The pressure should be on the inside of the thumb and not on the flat, palm side. It is important to point out that with this thumb up grip, the whole thumb is not lying along the back of the racket. This faulty thumb up grip (Figure 1–5a, b) produces the same problems on low balls that an extreme grip of the forehand produces. I have seen more problems with players using this incorrect thumb up backhand than with any other grip. Therefore, I do not teach the thumb up grip to beginners, who continually use the wrong grip. Instead, without changing the hand position, I have them wrap the thumb around the handle to touch the second finger (Figure 1–6). As they become accustomed to the position, they can shift the thumb up if they prefer. The problem is great enough so that I encourage a shift to the Continental grip if a beginner continually shifts too far around and flattens the thumb. The Continental is better than an extreme thumb up grip. A player will roll the arm and slice a high ball, but with the Continental can still play all heights well, while it is virtually impossible to get low balls well using an extreme thumb up grip. The dropped racket head is characteristic of an improper grip, so faulty grips should be changed before poor habits are formed. The arm is on the front side of the body during the backhand swing, so that the contact point is opposite the front foot with the Continental grip and forward of the front foot with the Eastern grip.

SERVICE GRIPS

Many instructors start out teaching the Eastern forehand grip for serving, but I start with the Continental. The Continental grip will allow full hand action and allow the butt end to clear the wrist as the hand flexes. It also places the racket face at a desirable angle for swinging across the ball for spin. An advanced player often shifts to an Eastern backhand with the thumb around

FIG. 1–6
Eastern backhand, thumb down

when hitting an extreme spin serve, as this grip facilitates hitting across the ball while still keeping the racket face pointing in the proper direction. The beginner will generally place the hand behind the handle as in the extreme forehand, but this must be discouraged immediately. The service grip should never be further around behind the handle than the Eastern forehand.

VOLLEY AND HALF VOLLEY GRIPS

Because most balls volleyed and half volleyed are low, the ideal grip for both forehand and backhand is the Continental. The fact that the grip need not be changed (that is, it can be used for forehand or backhand) is helpful when quick exchanges are played. This applies to both men and women, but most women do not have the wrist strength that a Continental grip requires. Therefore, I teach the grip that produces the most solid and consistent volley. A solid and consistent approach volley and first volley while at the full net position are far more important than the quick exchanges of subsequent volleys. About 90 percent of women will have to use the Eastern forehand and backhand grips to get this effect. The percentage is just the opposite for men, most of whom adapt readily to the Continental grip.

chapter 2

GROUNDSTROKES

A body position that facilitates immediate reaction to the ball as it leaves the opponent's racket is essential (Figure 2–1). This ready position is the wide stance and crouch characteristic of many sports. Although the width of the stance may vary, the feet should be outside the hips to enable a sideways movement when needed. The bend in the legs and trunk should be sufficient to place the body weight towards the balls of the feet and allow the arms and racket to move freely in front of the body. Make sure the elbows are slightly forward of the hips. The racket should be placed dead center, pointing upward and across the net so that there is an equal distance to move for either a forehand or backhand. Some people like to point the racket across the body toward the backhand side, because it is impossible to point it forward if they retain the Eastern backhand grip after hitting a backhand. I teach a return to the center position every time, loosening the right-hand grip and maintaining complete control of the racket with the left hand on the racket throat. I place great emphasis on being in the ready position on time, because many stroke problems stem from failure to get into the ready position.

9

Backswing

The backswing must be started as soon as the opponent hits the ball. A rushed forward swing often is the result of a delayed start. Movement of the racket, initiated with the left hand, and turning of the right foot must be simultaneous (Figure 2–2). The left hand is in control until the racket is about halfway back and the right foot has turned sideways without stepping backwards. I like to see the strings fully, as the racket is moving backwards, from the position across the net. The direction of the arm during the backswing should not be high and looping, but straight back. The straight-back backswing almost always results in a slight cir-

**FIG. 2–1
Ready position**

**FIG. 2–2
Start of the forehand pivot**

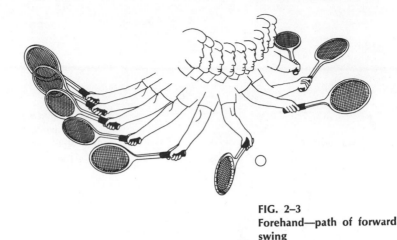

**FIG. 2–3
Forehand—path of forward
swing**

cular swing unless the ball is struck exactly at the height of the
starting position. Therefore, when the ball is waist high or lower,
the racket drops slightly when in the back position and the arm
follows the path of a flattened loop (Figure 2–3). To hit high balls,
the player draws the racket back high and the arm movement
forward is downward, producing a slice (backspin). The variations
are so numerous that a straight-back motion simply allows a
player to adapt to the variations. I do not attempt to groove
everyone into a definite pattern, but simply to eliminate excessive
raising of the racket at the start of the backswing or excessive
movement outward rather than backward, which might cause a
delay or rushing of the swing.

The angle between the racket and forearm varies in the ready
position, and will vary during the backswing (Figure 2–4a). The
main concern is to stop the exaggerated circular swing that starts
the racket upwards and back and requires the completion of a
full circle regardless of the speed of the oncoming ball. I teach
the straight-back movement because most swings will have a
slight circle, but the movement is controlled enough to allow a
player to limit the length of the backswing easily so as to retain
an unhurried forward swing.

The length of the backswing will depend on the speed of the
ball: the faster the ball approaches, the shorter the backswing.
The objectives are to hit the ball while retaining good body balance and to hit it at a chosen point of contact. This can only be
done if the entire movement is unhurried and the backswing precisely controlled.

FIG. 2–4
Sedgeman
forehand

a. Sedgeman cocks the racket up while taking the arm straight back.

b. The racket head is dropped just as the forward swing begins, and as the weight moves onto the front foot.

c. The shift of weight to the front foot has been completed, the racket handle is parallel to the ground, and the whole racket is almost at the bottom of the loop to facilitate moving upward during ball impact.

d. The forehand immediately after impact, with the racket head dropped only slightly. Note how trunk rotation allows freedom for the arm swing.

e. The racket is now slightly higher than the impact point, with both body rotation and arm swing continuing.

f. The racket points out across the net with the body in good balance.

The grip will dictate the point of contact, the angle of the racket face will determine the ball direction, and the direction and speed of the swing will give spin to the ball. For controlled forehands, topspin is most effective, so the racket must be moving upward during the impact (Figures 2–4, 2–5). The racket handle should be parallel to the ground, so that ball direction is controlled by the angle of the racket face. A little drop of the racket head is permissible, but no greater than in Figure 2–6b. Figure 2–6 shows the baseline view of Sedgeman's forehand. The whole racket is lower than the ball before impact and higher after impact, thus moving upward during contact. The higher the ball is contacted above the ground, the more difficult it is to hit with topspin. A downward swing becomes necessary for balls chest high or above using an Eastern grip, and waist high or above using a Continental grip.

Turning the right foot and stepping onto the left foot turns the body sideways, and the movement onto the front foot occurs

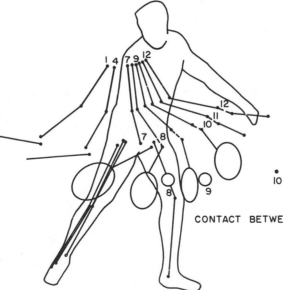

TENNIS FOREHAND

CONTACT BETWEEN 8 AND 9

FIG. 2–5
Sideview, forehand
composite: a frame-
by-frame tracing from
motion pictures

**FIG. 2–6 a, b, c
Sedgeman's forehand
from the back court**
(partially open stance)

just prior to the start of the forward swing (see Figure 2–4b). At this full back position the elbow is slightly bent and the hand extended backward forming an angle of approximately 45° with the line of the forearm, and with the racket face perpendicular to the ground. Figure 2–7a shows a 60° angle, and Figure 2–7b shows an angle of 30° at contact. This allows the body to act in sequence from the front leg, to the rotation of the trunk, to the arm swing, and finally a flexing of the hand (Figures 2–7b and 2-8). It is very important, however, to have the wrist set firmly by contact with no further flexing of the hand after contact, and very little during the follow-through. This is to assure racket control at impact without the stiff muscular swing that would result from a completely locked elbow and wrist.

Footwork is very important, to enable the full use of the body. So many shots are hit with an open stance that some instructors question the conventional body turn with the weight on the front foot. To use the entire body to its fullest, the body should be turned whenever possible with a shift of weight onto the left foot. This allows a forward shift of the legs and trunk prior to impact so the properly timed deceleration of each body segment in sequence can take place. This linking action of the body is the most efficient way of developing racket head velocity without using excessive muscle power.

The open stance is used mainly when a player must move to the right and does not have time to make the last step. The right

FIG. 2–7
Forehand top view at contact

a. The back position of the forehand is shown in a top view.

b. Note the amount of shoulder rotation and movement of the arm in relation to the shoulders. The racket forearm angle change indicates the extent of hand flexion.

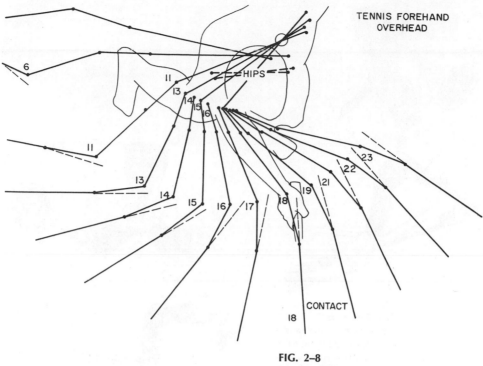

TENNIS FOREHAND
OVERHEAD

HIPS

CONTACT

FIG. 2–8
Forehand top view—a frame-by-frame tracing from motion pictures

foot hits last, balance is maintained, and the swing is executed. A good return can be made in an open stance because the trunk rotation and arm swing can still be executed smoothly and the player can obtain sufficient racket momentum (Figure 2–9). An open stance makes it easier to slice with a free-swinging follow-through, especially when only a short backswing is required. Accuracy is more important than power, so an open stance in good balance will produce the desired return better than a hurried, off-balance shot made while trying to get the left foot in a forward position. Although the open stance is often the result of a defensive position, it allows many winners to be hit as well. An important factor influencing stance is the height of the ball at impact.

I am adamant about teaching footwork to keep a player from retreating. A player should be in good balance on his front foot on every shot possible (Figure 2–10). I discourage back-stepping or running backward in an attempt to get the ball set up at a desired swing height. Most players who do this are caught off balance on the back foot and can manage only weak returns. The

**FIG. 2–9 a, b
Open stance forehand—**
Osuna, pulled wide to the
side, must swing with
the weight on the right
foot with the backswing
considerably shortened

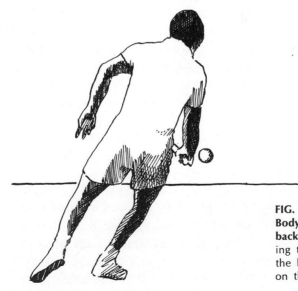

**FIG. 2–10
Body weight control,
backhand—**Seixas meet-
ing the ball early to hit
the ball with the weight
on the front foot

ball must be hit at whatever height it happens to be when it arrives at your contact point. You can adjust this height when the opponent hits the ball by turning in place or going forward; but to move backward, stop, and move onto the front foot is too time consuming. This means playing the ball at or slightly before the peak on balls that are hit short to you, or playing it on the rise with varying lengths of backswing as it hits closer to you. Under all circumstances, however, hit the ball in your strongest position. Teaching this from the first day a child holds a racket not only makes it easier to teach better ground strokes, but also helps in teaching the approach to the net, the return of service, and the volley.

The length of the follow-through will vary with the speed of the swing. The direction of the follow-through should be across the net for as long as possible, to assure control during impact (see Figure 2–4f). Beginners often pull across the body, swinging toward the sideline rather than across the net, thus hitting either a misdirected or a glancing shot. Control of the follow-through insures a longer flat area around the contact point, making errors less likely to occur if the timing is off slightly.

When the swing is finished, the left foot pulls back level with the right foot into the ready position. Controlling the right foot is extremely important, and any movement forward during the forward swing must be eliminated. Its movement rotates the right side of the body, partially interfering with the sequence of movements of the body parts as well as reducing the arm swing relative to the shoulders. When teaching, I often cure a multitude of faults merely by correcting a straying back foot. If a player is going to the net following the forehand, he brings the right foot forward for the first step, but must time this so as not to interfere with the forehand stroke.

This emphasis on footwork and balance and an unhurried swing, and discouragement of hitting a ball on the drop, makes practice on a wooden backboard undesirable. Using a backboard, if you stand close enough to hit the ball at the peak of the bounce or before, recovery of the follow-through is rushed abnormally. If the swing is unhurried, the ball must be hit low on the drop. Players who use a backboard are generally the ones who go deep behind the baseline, drop the racket head, and wait for the low ball that they like. They are also the ones who cannot get up to the net in doubles, because they have not learned to hit the ball on the rise. Although it may be fun to hit a backboard, there is no substitute for getting on the tennis court.

The backhand is a mirror image of the forehand in footwork and racket swing direction. There are several points of difference, however. The left hand takes the racket all the way back instead of halfway, and the grip is changed during the backswing (Figure 2–11a). Because the swinging arm is on the front side of the body, the contact point is forward of the front foot.

There are two other significant points that must be understood for proper execution. The body is in the way of the backswing, which is not true on the forehand side, so proper footwork and rotation of the shoulders is essential to obtain the proper back position (Figure 2–11b). There is also a natural arm roll with the racket face opening upward that does not occur on the forehand

FIG. 2–11
Backhand back-swing

a. The racket moves straight back with the left hand in control as the right hand moves to the proper grip. The left foot turn is simultaneous with the movement of the racket.

b. The body is turned so the back is visible from across the net, the right elbow is close of the middle of the abdomen, and the shift of weight onto the right foot has begun by the time the racket is fully back.

FIG. 2–12
Sedgeman backhand roll before impact

a. The roll of the arm in the full back position.

b. The levelling off of the swing and the flattening of the racket face before impact.

c. Position of impact with the shoulders perpendicular to the net.

(Figure 2–12a). Figure 2–12 shows the roll before contact. This latter difference between the forehand and backhand must be fully recognized for good results. The difference in the wrist action of the two strokes is especially noteworthy. The wrist remains straight during the backhand with only a slight cocking toward the thumb due to the fact that shoulder and forearm roll dominate in the swing. The forehand shows a definite break (extension) in the wrist due to the strength of the hand flexors used on the forward swing (see Figure 2–8). If this motion were duplicated on the backhand, the back of the hand would be moving directly into the ball and the wrist would be flexed in the full back position. Anatomically this is a much weaker body position than the normal backhand motion. Therefore, the roll and the hand position on top of the handle at impact is preferable for a smoother forward swing and greater firmness at impact. Many beginners take the racket back too high with a shortened body turn. This generally produces a swing that moves off to the right sidelines prematurely instead of across the net. This high backswing also makes it difficult to teach a topspin backhand, as the racket is in a perfect position for a slice. A full turn with the left hand in control all the way back is necessary to bring the racket straight back in preparation for hitting with topspin (Figure 2–13). Just prior to the forward swing of the racket, check

**FIG. 2–13
Topspin back-
hand**

b. The racket and left foot have made the initial move simultaneously.

a. The whole body is just coming down to the ready position so a turn can be made in either direction.

c. The backhand grip
is now in position,
and the right foot is
ready to step forward.

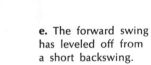

e. The forward swing
has leveled off from
a short backswing.

d. The weight is being
shifted to the right
foot, and the racket
head begins to drop.

FIG. 2–13 cont'd.

f. The weight is mostly on the front foot, and the racket has dropped lower than the ball height.

g. The contact point is forward of the front foot, the racket head is at the desirable angle, and the shoulders have remained perpendicular to the net.

h. The body position is similar to the contact point, but the arm swing continues, with the racket following the ball as long as possible.

i. The pointing of the racket across the net has been completed, and the recovery is about to start.

j. The racket was allowed to continue high and across the body. The weight is being transferred back to the left foot, so the right foot can recover backward.

k. The racket is about to be pulled back into the ready position, and the right foot has been pulled back almost level with the left.

the right elbow, as the arm should be back sufficiently to place the elbow near the middle of the abdomen and slightly away from the body (see Figure 2–11a). Rolling out to a "flat" racket position by impact will assure good ball control (Figures 2–14 and 2–15).

TENNIS

BACKHAND

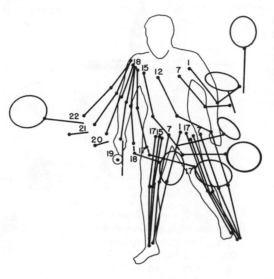

**FIG. 2–14
Sideview backhand
composite:** a frame-by-frame tracing from motion pictures

**FIG. 2–15
Gonzales—low back-
hand**

a. The right step had to be made toward the sideline and the roll out is about to begin.

b. The arm and racket are lowering during the arm swing.

c. Contact is made forward of the right foot with the swing almost level through the contact area. The shoulders are perpendicular to the net at contact.

d. The follow-through is slightly restricted because of the position of the right foot, but the swing continues to point across the net. Note the diagonal thumb position, the hand on top of the racket.

The follow-through should have good direction if the sideways position of the shoulders is maintained until after impact (Figure 2–16). Obtaining a proper back position is a difficult movement for many beginners. Once the full turn is mastered, concentration should be primarily on the arm swing. The arm should immediately move away from the trunk, starting its forward swing as soon as the front foot is set. A major problem for beginners is insufficient arm swing before contact, with too great an emphasis on trunk rotation. This results in a racket swing produced mainly from the legs and trunk. Any exaggerated turn of the trunk misdirects the swing and also fails to aid the arm swing with a properly timed deceleration. The result is the flinging motion off to the sidelines characteristic of some beginners. To teach proper arm swing, concentrate on not letting the shoulders go beyond the line perpendicular to the net. If I encounter difficulty, I stand behind the player and hold the left shoulder, thus restricting the turn. The unencumbered freedom of the follow-through presents no problems as long as the line of the shoulders is controlled. The length and height of the forward swing will vary with its speed and direction, respectively (Figure 2–17).

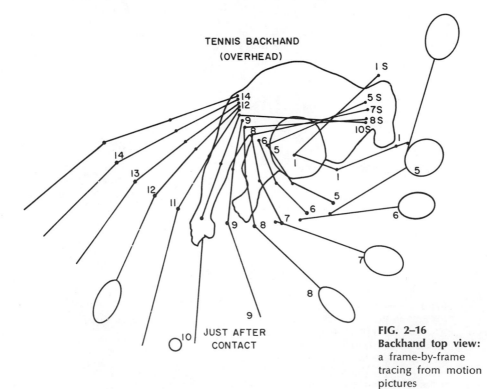

TENNIS BACKHAND
(OVERHEAD)

JUST AFTER
CONTACT

**FIG. 2–16
Backhand top view:**
a frame-by-frame
tracing from motion
pictures

**FIG. 2–17
Santana—backhand
ace**

a. The pivot has started, with the right foot ready to step forward.

b. The weight is being shifted to the right foot, and the racket head has started its drop during a very controlled backswing.

c. The swing is levelling out with the body in perfect position.

d. Contact is made forward of the right foot with the shoulders almost perpendicular to the net.

FIG. 2–17 cont'd.

e. The arm swing con-
tinues as the body
remains in place. The
racket swing was level
through impact, indicat-
ing very little spin was
imparted due to the
swing.

f. The body is still
close to its position
at impact, indicating
the full arm swing
that took place. The
racket face turns up as
the shoulder maintains
a position of non-
stress.

g. This high position is
an indication of the
smoothness of the
stopping motion of a
vigorous swing.

Ball direction and speed after impact are determined by several factors: the angle of the racket face at impact; the speed, weight, flexibility, and center of gravity of the racket; the speed, spin, and angle of approach of the ball before impact; and the firmness of the grip at impact. The player has chosen the racket he prefers and should always try to hit the ball in the center of the strings with a firm grip, so that all that is left for him to control is the angle of the racket face and direction of the swing.

The racket face must be held firmly at the desired angle at impact. If the ball is moving rapidly upward with topspin, the racket face must be aimed toward the top of the net or even into the net to keep the ball from going long. If the ball is near the top of the bounce, the racket face will be approximately perpendicular to the ground, but must vary according to the speed and direction of the swing (Figure 2–18). The slower the swing or the

MOMENTUM CONSIDERED TO OBTAIN TRUE BALL VELOCITY
AFTER IMPACT

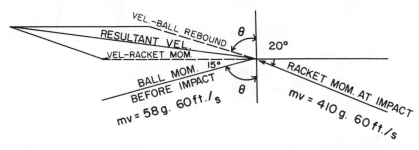

FIG. 2–18.
Ball direction, after impact, determined from racket face angle, racket swing direction, and the ball direction before impact.

more topspin you put on the ball, the more the face is opened upward. This racket face angle is maintained as long as it is comfortable, before and after impact, to assure accuracy. Even though a roll of the racket is evident during the entire swing, the racket should not roll through the impact area (Figure 2–19).

It is very important to realize that the racket face angle is not

*Ground-
strokes*

**FIG. 2–19 a, b, c, d
Forehand—level swing
through contact area,**
with an extreme roll over,
during follow-through

changed to produce topspin in any stroke (Figure 2–20). If a
great deal of topspin is desired, the swing angle must be increased upward. With the arm going high on the follow-through,
a turn or roll at the shoulder maintains an anatomically neutral
position; however, this roll takes place after impact. If the roll

**FIG. 2–20
Laver—topspin forehand**

a. Laver is dropping the racket low
to enable the swing to move
upward sharply. This slight-face
down position is typical when
the shoulders are not turned fully.
Some beginners do this when
learning a normal forehand, and
the shoulder rotation must be
corrected.

b. The racket is almost
at its lowest point.

c. The racket face is
flattening just before
impact.

FIG. 2–20 cont'd.

d. The racket face is perpendicular to the ground during impact, with the racket moving upward.

e. The racket face is still perpendicular while the swing continues upward.

f. The high point of the swing is reached with the racket face still perpendicular to the ground.

g. The final rolling of the racket is only to ease the shoulder joint stress.

occurs too early, it will affect the area of impact so that more shots will be missed. The velocity of the racket head through the impact area is so fast that the eye cannot distinguish what is actually happening. Many people believe topspin is obtained by rolling the racket, because it is possible to see a change in the racket face at the beginning and end of the swing and they assume it was continuous. When teaching beginners, I emphasize the flat racket during the entire swing, with allowances for slight changes to eliminate any abnormal muscular stress. It is important to stop beginners from forcibly rolling the racket to attain topspin.

chapter 3

THE VOLLEY

When the player is standing near the net, the ready position is very important because he has less time to react. This ready position is similar to a back court ready position, but the racket must be held a bit lower and more forward. The crouch should also be lower, and the elbows well forward of the hips. This position prepares a player for the low, hard shot.

I have found that most people stand too close to the net when volleying, and too close to the sideline when playing doubles. A player should try to position himself for the best total court coverage and for strong volleys. The area just inside the service line to halfway between the net and service line is where most volleying takes place (Figure 3–1). If you approach this position from the back court, the first volley generally occurs in an area between the service line and two yards behind (Figure 3–2). This is the so-called "no man's land," which is an unfortunate term because any player who goes to the net in singles or doubles must learn to hit the first volley in this area. If you stop to make the volley in good balance, this is as far forward as you can get in the time available (Figure 3–3). The second volley is made inside the service line in the preferred net position (Figure 3–4). A grass surface requires a net rushing game, and almost every point contains a mid-court volley. Playing a net rushing game also reduces greatly the number of forehands and backhands

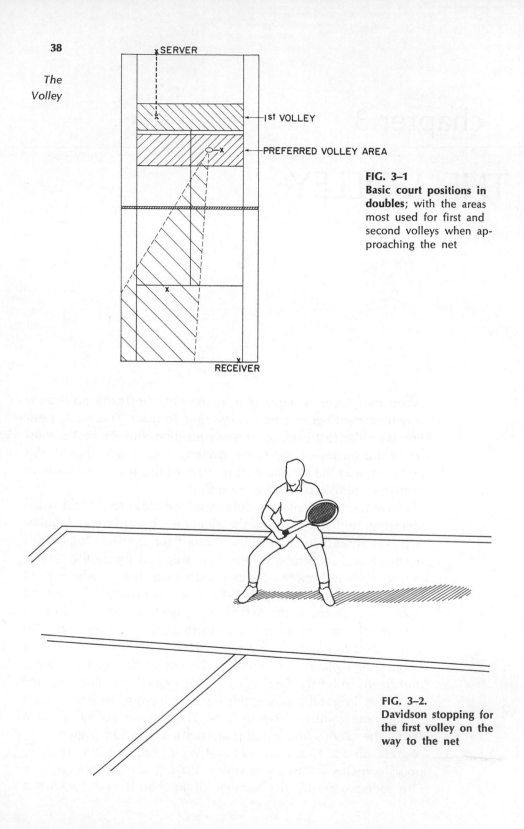

**FIG. 3–1
Basic court positions in
doubles**; with the areas
most used for first and
second volleys when ap-
proaching the net

**FIG. 3–2.
Davidson stopping for
the first volley on the
way to the net**

FIG. 3–3
Gonzales, having stopped behind the service line, is about to move to his left for the first volley.
After making the volley, he will continue inside the service line for the second volley

FIG. 3–4
Second volley position—
Position reached is a balanced position ready for the second volley

from the baseline, other than the return of service. As the surface changes, the need for ground strokes changes, and most of the tennis playing public play on slower surfaces. This fact does not lessen the importance of the mid-court shot, the practice of which should not be neglected. On a slower court there is slightly more time to get closer to the net, and if the move is properly executed a player should get nearly to the service line.

The partner of the server in doubles should also stand in a position that allows good court coverage. He should stand half to three quarters of the way back from the net to the service line, and about halfway between the center line and the singles side-line (see Figure 3–1). His prime concern is the ball through the middle of the court; overconcern for protecting the alley will cause the server undue hardship, because he will be required to cover three quarters of the court. It is difficult to teach players to become more active at the net, and thus to cover more court and confound, antagonize, and outguess the receiver. Best results can be obtained only by getting out of the corner.

Regarding footwork, anything is acceptable as long as the racket firmly meets the ball. One should turn sideways by step-ping forward with the opposite foot (Figure 3–5). The only unac-ceptable movement is stepping forward with the near foot, which counters the proper shoulder turn. This movement has no advan-tage and takes as much time as stepping with the opposite foot. It is very often impossible to take a full step forward, so a turn of the shoulders with no step, a sideways step with the near foot,

FIG. 3–5
Trabert—turning for a backhand volley; note right foot step and racket handle parallel to ground

a pivot away with the near foot, or other small variations will get the racket on the ball on time (Figures 3–6 and 3–7).

Another common fault is to hit off balance with the weight back. To obtain good body balance it is important that you always go forward from the ready position to meet the ball (Figure 3–8).

FIG. 3–7
Laver—pivoting in place for a low backhand volley

FIG. 3–6
Laver—stepping sideways with the near foot while turning the shoulders for a backhand volley

FIG. 3–8
High backhand volley met forward of the body. The arm is in a strong position with the racket angled upward. Beginners tend to raise the elbow to shoulder level when hitting a high ball, resulting in a weak volley

The swing is limited and is controlled according to the time available and speed of the approaching ball. Standing near the net will allow only a short swing or practically none at all. The faster the ball, the shorter the swing. A slow ball requires a slight backswing to get sufficient ball speed on the return (Figure 3–9).

**FIG. 3–9
Sedgeman—forehand
volley**

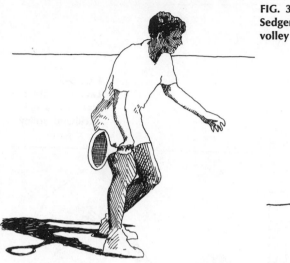

a. Time was not available to move the feet, so the body was rotated and the backswing limited.

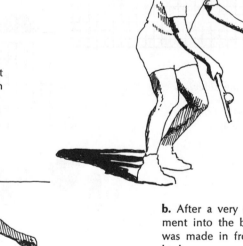

c. The firmness of the grip and rigidity of the whole body at contact result in no follow-through. Although the arm has moved forward slightly, the racket has bounced backward slightly.

b. After a very short movement into the ball, contact was made in front of the body.

This swing during a volley differs from that for a ground stroke in that the wrist is never cocked in the volley (Figure 3–10). The movement is more of a whole arm movement, with the wrist rigid at all times. The slight open face characteristic of the backhand may also occur, but the racket must roll out flat in time for contact. Any exaggeration of this open face will cause errors.

In doubles play, the partner of the receiver must choose where to stand. He can take the full net position (when confident of his partner's return) or play a modified position, which would not make the team as vulnerable if the opponent at the net picks off the return of the service. This modified position is near the service line in the middle of the area of the best return (see Figure 3–1). This position is played by the server's partner to counter the pick-off, and should the return pass the net player, the position is changed to a full net position immediately. It is not uncommon to see this modified position taken during the first

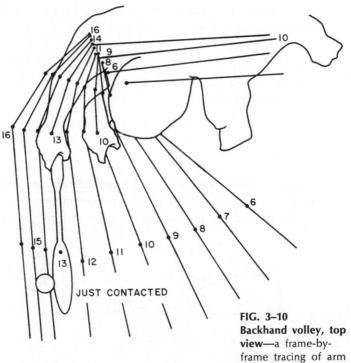

JUST CONTACTED

**FIG. 3–10
Backhand volley, top
view**—a frame-by-
frame tracing of arm
and racket movement
during a backhand
volley, showing
shoulder stability

service, and the full net position taken for the second service.

The most difficult volley to teach is the approach volley (the first volley made on the way forward to the full net position). Not only is it likely to be low, but it is difficult to stop in balance and on time. The server must move forward while the ball is in flight to the receiver. As the receiver hits the ball, the server must be stopped with feet spread, ready to react to the direction of the return. The time available from the moment the server hits the ball until the receiver hits it is about 3/4 second for a first serve and 1 second for a second serve. If the server tries to make it forward to inside the service line, with no regard to getting set for the return, he will usually be caught moving forward and will not be able to move in a sideways direction if necessary. Therefore, by protecting against the low ball to the feet by moving fully forward, you are restricted in your court coverage and thus are more likely to err on the shot. There is no guarantee that you will not get a ball at your feet no matter where you are standing, even if you remain on the baseline. This timed stopping, whatever your court position, is absolutely essential to good volleying. Temporary stopping into a spread position takes place on almost every shot. It is evident not only on the approach volley but also during the return of serve and ground strokes. It is always timed to occur when the ball is contacting the opponent's racket.

HALF VOLLEY

If you are playing mid-court shots and not retreating on deep ground strokes, you will find yourself hitting more half volleys than when playing from 3 to 6 feet behind the baseline. The half volley should be slightly easier than a low volley if contact is

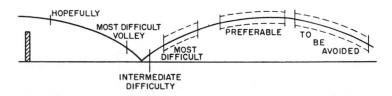

FIG. 3–11
Difficulty of areas of contact, showing: (1) The desired volley height; (2) The difficulty of a low volley; (3) The preference of a half volley over a ball hit on the rise close to the bounce; (4) The preferred area of contact just before the peak.

made immediately after the bounce. The force of impact on the racket is reduced due to the bounce, and the ball will go up and over the net more easily owing to the angle of bounce upward from ground to racket. The hardest shot in tennis remains that in which the ball is hit on the rise at that phase of the bounce where spin and bounce have affected the flight, but time for racket adjustment is not available (Figure 3–11). Therefore, the half volley must be made as close to the bounce as possible. It is important to practice these necessary mid-court shots and stop thinking of this area as a place to avoid.

chapter 4

THE SERVICE

INITIAL RACKET MOTION AND BALL TOSS

One of the great joys in tennis is serving the ace; one of the great disappointments is to double fault. Although ball speed is important in winning points, a good server varies the speed, spin, and placement of the serve. Methods of serving vary, but the fundamentals of the whole movement remain largely the same. The stance is taken so that a line drawn through the heels will point in the direction of the ball flight (Figure 4–1). The racket is pointed along this line with the racket face perpendicular to the ground, and the ball is held touching the strings (Figure 4–2). I discourage holding the racket throat with the last two fingers of the left hand, as this may cause a ball shift in the fingers after the movement begins. Both hands move downward together, separate, and move upward at the same rate. The left hand goes down to the inside of the thigh without touching the leg, and moves back upward in approximately the same plane as the downward movement. The arm continues upward to a position where the fingers point toward the ball, so that the eye, fingertips, and ball are in a straight line as the ball reaches its peak. Not all players keep the left hand in this forward position on the toss. Most tournament players move the left arm upward at a 90° angle to this plane, or off toward the sideline (Figure 4-3). They do this because of the extreme body rotation they use in hitting a hard

*The
Service*

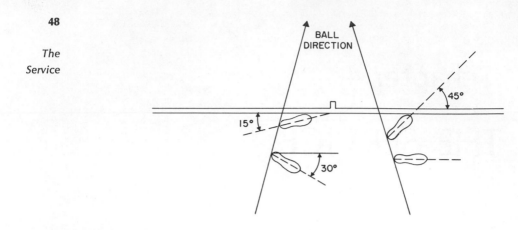

BALL
DIRECTION

45°

15°

30°

FIG. 4–1
Service—foot place-
ment

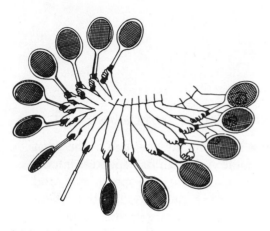

FIG. 4–2
Service backswing—starting
motion of the serve, with the
racket pointing at the service
court and the half turn of the
racket face during the backswing.

FIG. 4–3
**Newcombe—position of
left hand during the up-
ward motion on the toss**

ball (Figure 4–4). However, I have found that beginners have a more consistent toss and learn more quickly the basics of serving if they do not try to hit hard, do not attempt an extreme shoulder turn, and return the left arm upward in the plane of the downward movement (toward the net). The path of the left arm is controlled by the shoulders, and the comfort and naturalness of the motion should be the determining factor. The ultimate goal must be a consistent toss.

FIG. 4–4
Roche—service, rear view

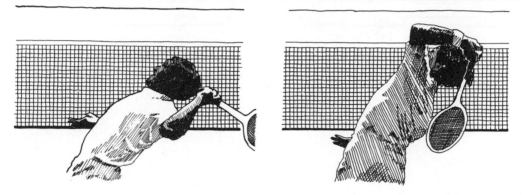

a. The shoulders are rotated fully and are perpendicular to the net.

b. The elbow is high, with the racket head still down the middle of the back.

c. The racket is moving toward the ball from the inside.

d. The contact point does not have the arm and racket at full reach. This allows the racket to move up and across the ball with good muscular control, and with less chance of joint injury.

e. The racket has moved across to the outside after contact

f. Inward rotation of the shoulder following contact is a natural motion to reduce joint stress.

The racket makes a circle starting a half turn when it is pointing at the ground (see Figure 4–2). By the time the racket is shoulder high, it is pointing directly backward, with the racket face perpendicular to the ground (see Figure 4–2). The striking face is on the left at the beginning, and is facing right while in the back position. Many players develop a pick-up from the starting position, and never point the racket straight down or straight back. Extreme shortness of preparation before the hitting motion begins is characteristic of Rosewall (Figure 4–5). He moves his

**FIG. 4–5
Rosewall—service**

a. The left hand and racket move downward together to this position and then start upward together in a pick-up rather than a looping motion.

b. The arms continue moving upward together.

c. The weight is shifting to the front foot, the racket head is about to drop down behind the back, and the ball is still going upward.

d. The ball is at its peak and the arm action is just starting.

FIG. 4–5 cont'd.

e. The hand remains fully cocked while the elbow is straightening.

f. The final sequence of body action shows the completion of the hand action prior to impact, with the swing moving across the ball.

g. The characteristic hip angle indicates the proper use of the trunk to aid the arm action.

h. Both feet are close together, indicating the controlled forward motion of the whole body. Compare with Newcombe (Fig. 4–7i), who has more forward motion before as well as after impact.

i. Although the ball was contacted above the baseline, and the arm is moving across the ball at about 45°, this is a first service. This shows that mixing serves is as important as hitting at high speeds, as Rosewall is one of the slowest servers in professional tennis.

hands in unison upward and arrives at the full cocked position with excellent racket control. One characteristic of the full body motion that I discourage is letting the wrist break in the wrong direction before it is cocked behind the back (Figure 4–6). This motion whips the racket into a full cocked position, but tends to loosen the grip and add to the control problem.

FORWARD SWING TO IMPACT

After the racket has reached the straight back position, the arm continues upward and the elbow bends to place the racket down the back (Figure 4–7). This motion into the extreme cocked position coincides with the start of the shift of weight forward, so that the shift of body weight has started forward before the cocking of the arm and racket is completed. The throwing motion then follows, with the arm reaching upward as it straightens. The sequence of this throwing action is best understood from the

FIG. 4–6
**Chaffee—the wrist break in the wrong
direction during the serving motion**

FIG. 4–7 Newcombe— service

a. The racket points at the service court; stance is wide, and weight about equally distributed on each foot.

b. The left hand moves down to the thigh together with the downward movement of the racket, and the weight shifts to the back foot.

c. The racket head starts its half turn at this point as both arms start upward.

d. The hands continue the upward motion at the same level, as the weight shift to the front foot has started.

FIG. 4–7 cont'd.

e. The bent front leg, the shoulder rotation, and the start of the racket movement behind the back are all in preparation for the forward swing.

f. The weight shift and leg straightening are completed, and the trunk is now performing its part as the arm is fully cocked.

g. The arm has completed its straightening and the hand is in its motion. Newcombe's vigorous forward motion has resulted in his feet leaving the ground and moving forward.

h. Contact is above the right shoulder, but well forward of the baseline. Newcombe hits the ball at the peak of the throw, requiring a fast overall motion.

i. The hard-hit first serve has the racket moving off to the right, with the right foot already taking the first step for the approach to the net.

j. The body balance is perfect at the completion of the follow-through as the net approach begins.

illustrations (Figure 4–8). Figure 4–8d shows the high elbow due to the motion of the upper arm; Figure 4–8e shows the movement due mainly to the forearm, with the upper arm having decelerated and remaining almost in the position shown in Figure 4–8d. Figure 4–8f shows the extent of the hand motion just before impact and also the small amount of motion of the forearm.

FIG. 4–8
Davidson is serving up an ace with the left foot remaining in place throughout the swing with no movement forward into the court. This sequence of pictures shows the coordination between the body segments and the whip action from foot to hand.

a. The kneebend, backbend, and shoulder rotation take place as the racket is moving down behind the back.

b. The weight has shifted to the front foot, and body action is started before the racket reaches this full cock position.

c. Shoulder rotation and trunk angular motion is aiding the arm motion. Note that the elbow is moving up high, but there is no straightening at the elbow and wrist joint.

d. The upper arm has completed its movement and the forearm has started its movement.

e. The forearm has completed most of its movement, and the wrist joint is still cocked.

f. The hand motion has completed the whip action at contact. This slightly bent body position at impact is characteristic of all good servers. Always look for that jutting buttocks as a key to a well-coordinated body action.

g. The hitting face of the racket is turned outward just after impact to maintain a position of non-stress in the shoulder joint.

FIG. 4–8 cont'd.

h, i, j. The follow-through exhibits excellent body balance with a gradual slowing down of the racket.

Each body segment moving at the proper time, in sequence, produces the maximum racket head velocity. Because the trunk and legs are the heaviest parts of the body, they are also the most influential, even though the arm gives the greatest range of motion. I have found that a restriction of full body motion with emphasis on arm and hand motion allows faster progress for beginners. They tend to retain the basic sequence of action and have no problem moving through a fuller range of motion as they progress toward hitting a harder ball.

FOLLOW-THROUGH

The follow-through is generally across the body to the left, but will vary according to the racket swing direction to put spin on the ball (Figure 4–9). The best advice is to do what is most natural without any abrupt stopping.

FIG. 4–9
Molloy's long service
follow-through

Although there are certain fundamentals that must be learned, many variations meet with equal success. Variations characteristic of many good servers are seen in: 1) the path of the left arm, 2) the height of the toss, 3) the timing of the weight shift, 4) the racket path to get to the cocked position, 5) the amount of back bend and shoulder rotation, 6) the point at which the ball is struck in relation to both the server and court, 7) the speed of the whole movement, 8) the timing and use of the body segments, 9) the grip and its firmness at impact, and 10) direction and length of the follow-through.

The shift of weight forward before hitting varies with the height of the throw. The player can start the entire movement with the weight on either the front or back foot as long as the forward movement is properly timed. A fast swinger who hits the ball near the peak of the throw generally starts with the weight on the back foot, and begins the shift of body weight forward soon after the racket movement begins. For most people, I believe, this hurried swing is undesirable because it will result in less accuracy and control. As a player advances out of the "beginner" category, I do not discourage starting on the back foot as long as the start of the forward motion is timed so as not to interfere with a rhythmic, controlled motion.

OBTAINING BALL SPIN

I have all beginners start on the front foot and visualize a plane that includes the body and ball flight. If the swing of the racket remains in this plane, the serve will be hit flat with the racket face perpendicular to the line of ball flight. Actually, even a beginner will tend to hit across the ball slightly from the inside out, simply because the trunk is rotating and the racket is coming from behind the body. This motion across the ball is desirable, and absolutely necessary if the ball is hit hard. This slight angle of swing, usually about 15°, is termed a "slice" serve, which means that the direction of swing has gone off to the right of the ball flight direction (Figures 4–10, 4–11). The racket face is perpendicular to the intended ball flight, to obtain the correct ball direction. A serve hit with enough spin to make it visibly change direction when it hits in the service court is a "twist" serve. The terminology is somewhat arbitrary, but a twist serve would require an angle of swing of about 40°–60° across the ball line of

**FIG. 4–10 a, b
Composite—service
(overhead view),** angle
of swing across the
ball

1st SERVE

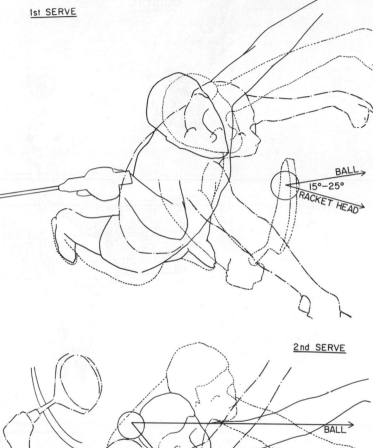

BALL
15°–25°
RACKET HEAD

2nd SERVE

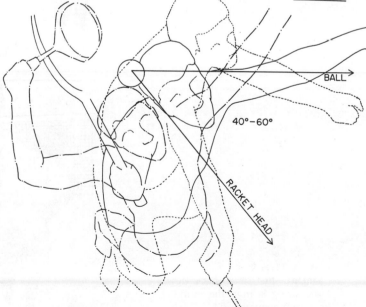

BALL
40°–60°
RACKET HEAD

FIG. 4–11 a, b, c
Santana—first serve, back view.
The swing is from the inside
out, approximately 35°

flight (Figures 4–10b and 4–12). As a player develops a hard serve, he hits the ball with varying amounts of spin. A ball is never hit flat at high speeds, because that way it could not be hit into the service court (see Appendix A). The first, hard serve

**FIG. 4–12 a, b, c
Santana—second serve,
back view.** The swing is
from the inside out,
approximately 60°

of a tournament player is generally hit with the racket moving across the ball at 15°, and the second serve has the racket head moving outward about 45° (Figures 4–13 and 4–14). As the angle across the ball increases, there is a corresponding increase of the

FIG. 4–13 a, b, c, d, e Sedgeman—first serve. A controlled body motion showing the direction of the follow-through. Compare with Figure 4–14, which shows an identical body motion

**FIG. 4–14 a, b, c, d, e
Sedgeman—second serve.** The
angle of the follow-through
indicates the difference between
first and second serves

upward movement of the racket head; therefore, a second serve is contacted slightly lower than is a first serve (Figures 4–15 and 4–16).

The height of the throw and the resulting drop distance before impact vary considerably. Table 4–1 shows the drop distance of selected players. I teach a drop of 6"–12" from the peak of the

FIG. 4–15 a, b, c
Osuna—first serve, (back view). The point of contact is to the right, with the racket straight up and the follow-through slightly to the right of the ball flight.

FIG. 4–16 a, b, c, d
Osuna—second serve. The point of contact is more to the left than on the first serve, the racket is angled slightly at contact, and the swing is considerably more across the ball to the outside than in the first serve

TABLE 4–1

HEIGHT OF THROW ABOVE THE CONTACT POINT AMONG SOME TOP TENNIS PLAYERS

0 – 1"	Newcombe, Grabner, Talbert
1"– 3"	Seixas, Savitt, Palafox, Emerson, Osuna, Pilic
3"– 5"	Ashe
6"– 9"	Gonzales, Sedgeman, Hoad, Laver, Roche
9"–12"	Kramer, Mulloy, Richardson, Rose, Rosewall (1969)
12"–15"	Stolle, Ralston, Smith, Santana, Connolly
15"–20"	Smith, MacKay, Rosewall (1952)
20"–24"	Lutz, Santana, Garcia, Drysdale, Barthe, Brough
24"–30"	Chaffee

**FIG. 4–17 a, b, c, d, e, f
Smith—first serve.** A view from across the net shows Smith's contact point in relation to his left foot, and his angle of swing across the ball

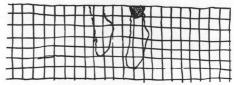

throw to the point of impact. This allows time for an unhurried backswing, a controlled cocking of the racket, and a smooth, rhythmic forward motion. The major problems for most tennis players are accuracy and consistency and not the development of more racket speed.

The position of the ball toss varies with the type of serve delivered. The slice is hit out in front of the body, about in line with the right shoulder (Figure 4–17). If more spin is desired, the racket must move across the ball at a greater angle, to direct more of the racket head velocity into the spin of the ball and less into ball velocity toward the opponent. This requires throw-

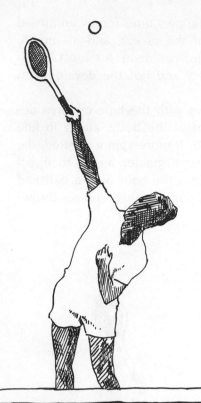

FIG. 4–17 cont'd.

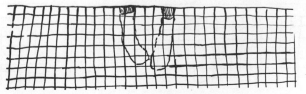

ing the ball more to the left and slightly back (Figures 4–18 and 4–19). The farther to the left the ball is thrown, the lower will be the contact point, to facilitate hitting the ball. This results in the racket head moving upward as well as sideways, causing a combination of topspin and sidespin of the ball. To put a lot of topspin and only a little sidespin on the ball, the throw would have to be about a foot or more to the left of the left foot, and the ball struck lower than normal. A ball hit with a lot of sidespin and a little topspin would be thrown to the right of the left foot and hit at a near normal height. This sidespin serve is used to pull an opponent off the court; it is placed near the outside line when the serve is to the right-hand court. This exaggerated sidespin causes the ball flight to curve, giving it a different angle of ap-

**FIG. 4–18 a, b, c, d
Smith—second serve.** A comparison with Smith's first serve shows the different point of contact and the increased angle of swing across the ball

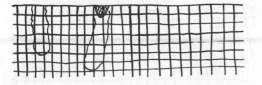
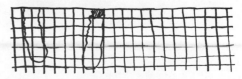

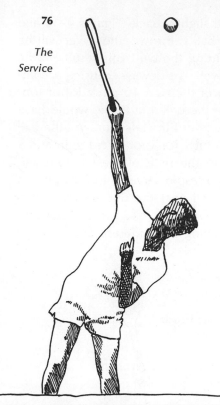

FIG. 4–18 cont'd.

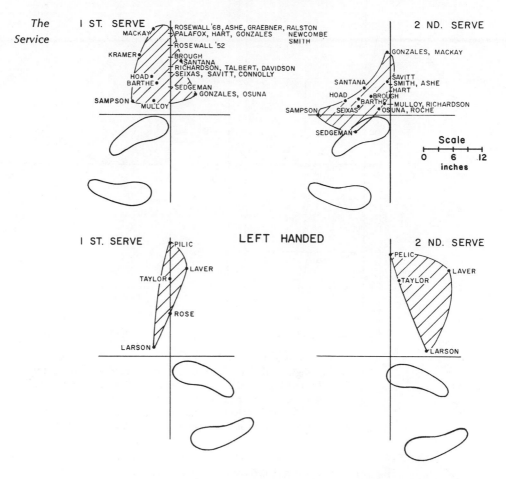

FIG. 4–19
Area of service toss. The shaded areas
indicate the difference in the position of the
toss between the first and second serves.
Occasionally a player is listed twice to
emphasize that a variety of serves are used

proach to the court (Figure 4–20). The spin will still make the
ball kick slightly to the right, but the over-all result is a wider
ball to the server's left. Many people believe a reverse spin is
used, but it is not. In good tennis there is no such thing as a
reverse spin, in which the racket is brought from the outside to
the inside of the line of ball flight.

The amount of ball drop during the flight from racket to court
depends on gravity, ball spin, ball velocity, height of impact,
angle of departure and wind conditions.

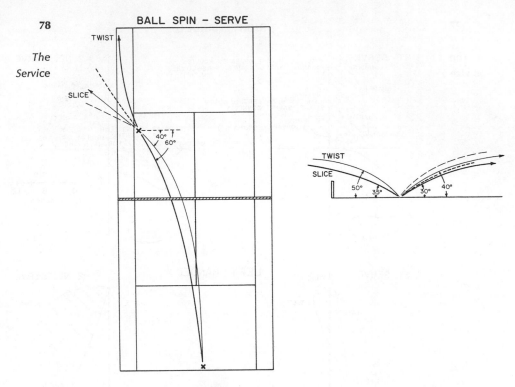

FIG. 4–20 a, b
Ball flight and bounce. A twist serve bounces more to the
right and higher than a slice serve. A slice serve with exaggerated side spin would be used to pull an opponent off the
court. This is due to the angle of approach to the bounce and
lesser amount of spin to cause deviation after the bounce.

The misconception that revolving the racket head around the
ball ("peeling the cover") will give spin is probably due to the
racket position early and late in the swing. As previously explained, angular ball velocity is obtained from the swing direction, racket head velocity, and angle of the racket face. The
racket face angle must be properly set by the time of impact.

ANATOMICAL VARIATIONS

Any change in racket head position after impact is due to joint
adjustments to retain a position of non-stress. The turn of the
racket face outward is the result of the anatomical structure of
the shoulder. As the arm is raised to an overhead position, the
body tries to retain a position of strength without undue mus-

cular stretching, so the upper arm remains in alignment with the shoulders (Figure 4–21). The shoulder is in a neutral position, with the palm of the hand toward the body when the arm is hanging down; with the palm forward when the arm is raised overhead; and with the palm downward when the arm is pointing backward. Shoulder and upper arm alignment are, therefore, very in-

FIG. 4–21 a, b
Graebner and Brough. A straight line is maintained from the elbow through both shoulders to keep the shoulder joint in a favorable position of strength during the swing

fluential on racket face positions. In addition, if the hand is flexed, a natural rotation of the hand due to the bone structure of the wrist turns the palm outward when the arm is overhead (Figure 4–22). This extreme hand flexion does not occur when serving, but occurs on an overhead smash when the lob is struck well behind the head.

FIG. 4–22
Wrist rotation for extreme hand flexion. Note: this position does not occur when serving. However, this outward turning of racket facilitates hitting a placement toward right side (opponent's left), when an overhead smash is contacted behind the body.

a. The forearm is stabilized and the hand extended over a stool.

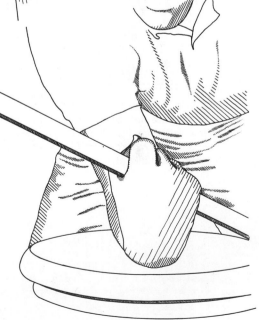

b, c. In the flexed position the stick rotates upward and backward.

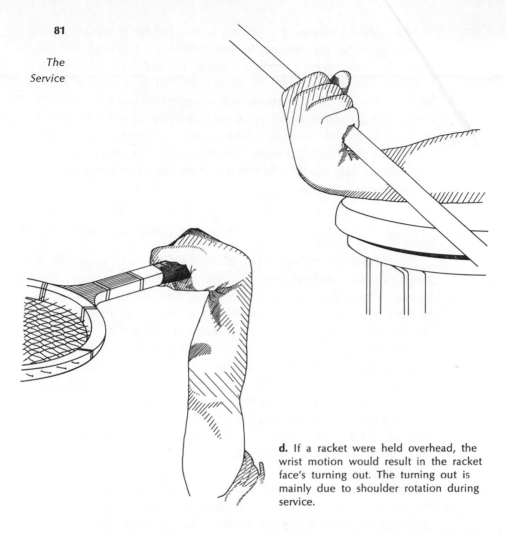

d. If a racket were held overhead, the wrist motion would result in the racket face's turning out. The turning out is mainly due to shoulder rotation during service.

The amount of racket head change varies with the individual, and the amount of racket head recovery from this outward turn varies with the length of the follow-through. A long follow-through to the left of the body is characteristic of the slice serve, whereas a short movement down to the right is characteristic of the twist serve. The more abrupt the stop, the more muscle is being used. Therefore, it is best to follow a path that allows a gradual deceleration of the swing. The over-all result is that the body is continually attempting to maintain a rhythmic, smooth motion and at the same time exert optimum muscular strength while eliminating unwanted stresses. Therefore, arm rotation does not aid in hitting the ball harder but is simply the natural result of a good swing.

Although it looks as though the ball is struck at full reach, it is important that the arm not be overstretched. A position of full reach with the elbow locked should be avoided. This overstretched position causes loss of control and is often the cause of shoulder and elbow strain. An exaggerated upward motion toward the ball, a very fast swing, or just trying to reach high will all result in this unfavorable position. The muscle and joint forces are tremendous during a serve, and the proper technique of serving will not only produce better accuracy and speed, but reduce the likelihood of injury.

THE BODY AS A LINK SYSTEM

The proper coordination of all the body parts produces a greater racket head velocity with less muscular effort than does an uncoordinated movement. A body segment is put into forward motion, and then its timed deceleration helps the forward motion of the next segment. This segment in turn decelerates to help the next, so that a chain reaction occurs to give the racket angular velocity. This explains the need for the shift of the weight forward at the beginning of the swing, and why the front foot is so important in obtaining full use of the whole body in all strokes. It also explains why the backward movement of the hips is an indicator of proper serving motion, or more exactly, why the angular trunk motion, as the whole body moves forward, is necessary for good serving (Figures 4–23, 4–24, and 4–25).

Inadequate shoulder rotation is a common problem, especially among women. Improper use of the trunk results in the typical throwing motion of a girl with the elbow pushed forward and the ball struck low. The key to controlling the body parts and obtaining good timing is to restrict forward motion and emphasize proper body movements.

The right foot step into the court is not necessary for good serving, as is illustrated by Davidson serving up an "ace" (see Figure 4–8). Many beginners hinder learning by bringing the right foot across the baseline early, falling off balance as they attempt the serve. The right foot step forward is only used to catch balance after the ball has been struck, and to facilitate the approach to the net. I teach beginners to serve without moving the back foot, but to keep the toe touching as the weight goes onto the front foot. When the body motion has been learned properly, a good serve will be retained and forward motion added. Some

FIG. 4–23 a, b, c, d
**Ralston serves with a
great deal of body lean,**
and has a very extreme
turn of the racket out-
ward after the impact.

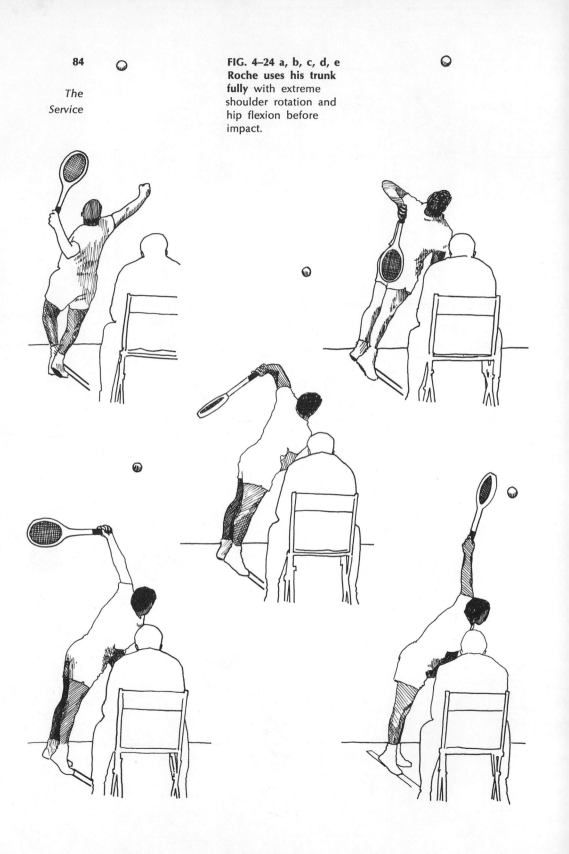

**FIG. 4–24 a, b, c, d, e
Roche uses his trunk
fully** with extreme
shoulder rotation and
hip flexion before
impact.

FIG. 4–25 a, b, c, d
**Ashe's serves are hard,
but controlled,** a result of
an unhurried, full motion,
and excellent position at
impact.

good servers occasionally fall into the bad habit of moving the weight early, thus falling out of control during the swing (Figure 4–26). If the body parts are not being used properly due to over-hitting or an early forward motion, the cure is to serve without the right foot step. Serving without crossing the baseline can correct problems of accuracy, dropping the head early, solidness at impact, and muscle soreness.

The trunk is the heaviest and the most influential body segment even though the arm and hand action has the fullest range. Every body part plays an integral role in ball speed, however, and each body segment is dependent on all the others.

The so-called "high elbow" position is important because the upper arm points upward (rather than forward as when throwing a ball) and the deceleration continues the link action to the fore-

**FIG. 4–26
Poor service contact position.** A premature body movement resulting in a foot fault as well as a poor serve.

arm and subsequently to the hand and racket. If the elbow and wrist are not fully cocked, an over-all arm action occurs, which requires greater muscle action at the shoulder. This not only causes undue stress but results in lower racket velocity at impact.

GRIP FIRMNESS

The final important factor in obtaining control and ball speed is the firmness of the grip at contact. A vigorous body motion, in attempting to reach high racket speeds, may very well result in less hand control, which will result in loss of ball speed and accuracy. Figure 4–27 shows the relationship between the ball speed, racket head velocity, and the striking mass. (Striking mass is dependent on grip firmness.) Several serves were measured

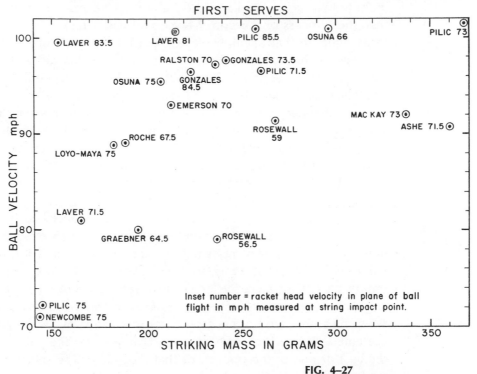

FIG. 4–27
Graph—the ball velocity attained by numerous top players resulting from the racket head velocity and grip firmness. The striking mass is a variable dependent on grip firmness.

from slow-motion pictures (64 frames per second, 1/4 open shutter) in the plane of the ball flight. The racket head linear velocity was measured at the point of impact of the strings both *before and after impact. The ball velocity after impact was measured, and the striking mass was calculated using the formula:*

$$\begin{array}{ccc} \text{Before Impact} & & \text{After Impact} \\ mV + mV & = & mV + mV \\ \text{ball} \quad \text{racket} & & \text{ball} \quad \text{racket} \end{array}$$

Because the velocities are measured, the coefficient of restitution need not be included in this formula. The striking mass varies with the firmness of the grip and can be less than the racket weight during poor contact, or greater than racket and hand weight during solid impact. Several conclusions from Figure 4–27 indicate that racket head speed developed is no more important than the firmness of the grip. Newcombe had a racket head velocity equal to that of other players, but hit this particular serve 25 miles per hour slower. Pilic hit two serves, which differed by almost 30 miles per hour, with the same racket head speed. Ashe and Pilic showed more ball speed, owing to good grip rather than fast racket speed. Osuna hit one serve 5 miles per hour faster than another of his serves, with a swing 9 miles per hour slower. Gonzales hit one serve 2 miles per hour faster than another serve, with a swing 11 miles per hour slower. Rosewall had the slowest racket speed; Laver, Gonzales, and Pilic were able to obtain the fastest racket head speed.

It is apparent from these data that it is not beneficial to have the racket contact point travelling faster than 70 to 75 miles per hour for consistent serving. A high racket velocity makes it difficult to hold the racket firmly, so nothing is gained by it. Concentration on greater racket velocity, however, could result in lack of control and sore muscles. It must be emphasized that the serves measured are not necessarily representative of the players presented. A specific serve measured may have been one of the best or one of the poorest of that individual. The serves are presented only to illustrate the relationship between the grip firmness and racket velocity. They emphasize that consistency, accuracy, and variation of serves will be improved if ball speed is not overemphasized.

chapter 5

RETURN OF SERVICE

The average player rallies from the baseline, goes to the net and volleys a few, hits a few serves to loosen up the overhead, and then begins play. The most neglected aspect of tennis is probably *practicing* the return of serve. Playing gives a great deal of exposure, but practice is just as important as it is in any other phase of tennis.

Although the return of a first serve may be waist high, a second serve must generally be hit near shoulder height. If a receiver moves in close enough to get the ball low, the speed of the ball and the time available to react to the bounce would result in many errors. To move back behind the baseline is to invite disaster, as the receiver is vulnerable to being pulled off the court as well as giving the opponent more time. Therefore, a return of serve is characterized by a shortened backswing, a raised racket head, and a downward swing (Figure 5–1). The slice is imperative on any high ball because of the difficulty of swinging upward. The ball bounces off the ground at a much greater angle than on a ground stroke, so the rebound from the racket will be increased upward. A serve usually has topspin, so the upward rebound will be further exaggerated. Because of these two factors it is necessary to aim a return toward the top of the net or lower just to keep the ball from going long on the return

**FIG. 5–1 a, b, c, d, e
Stolle—an offensive return
of a second serve** hit with a
slight slice, in perfect balance
on the front foot at impact,
and with a long controlled
follow-through.

(Figure 5–2). The high ball, the slicing motion, and the need to compensate for ball rebound make the return of serve quite different from most other ground strokes. Because of the short time factor and short backswing, concentration on grip firmness and on meeting the ball solidly will increase the accuracy of the returns. Many off-center hits occur when returning serves, and

FIG. 5–2 a, b, c, d, e
Smith—offensive return of a serve taken inside the baseline. Fig. c shows the racket face angle toward the net to compensate for the upward rebound off the racket. Because of the ball height the swing was almost level, and balance on the front foot was maintained throughout the forward swing.

they reduce ball velocity greatly. It is interesting to note, however, that ball direction is not changed from the original racket face angle, even though the racket may turn considerably (Figure 5–3).

The footwork should be quite varied, as good body balance is necessary for proper racket control. Due to the short time available for the return, an open stance is often required just to get

FIG. 5–3
Off center contact

a, b. A ball hit off center will turn the racket face, but the ball will continue in the direction dictated by the original position of the racket face.

c. The racket face returns to its original position.

the racket on the ball (Figure 5–4). Therefore, the essence of re-turning serves well is accurate and consistent placement, rather than speed. A well-hit return is likely to have good speed any-way, because the speed of the serve produces good rebound speed. Most receivers do a little two-step before the server hits the ball, trying to get set in a wide stance with the weight for-ward just as the server contacts the ball (see Figure 5–4a). This

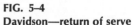

**FIG. 5–4
Davidson—return of serve**

a. The wide stance position is timed to coincide with the ball on the server's racket.

b. One step sideways with a short backswing was all that time allowed.

c. This is a defensive return of a first serve, as the ball is received deep and low with a slicing motion.

d. The typical follow-through; a short follow-through with the arm low.

position allows immediate reaction to the ball and increases the chance of meeting the ball in good balance. No matter how well grooved your swing or how much you know about the execution of a return, only sufficient practice against speed and variation will produce good results. Returning serves results in many variations on strokes, owing to height, speed, and spin differences. An individual's ability to make an offensive as well as a defensive return governs the receiver's court position as well as the speed of his return (Figures 5–5, 5–6, 5–7, 5–8, and 5–9).

**FIG. 5–5 a, b, c
Return of serve—**
Smith closes in for the
kill, but finds himself on
the defensive and slices
it back.

FIG. 5–6 a, b, c, d
Return of serve—Newcombe started
out in control, but found himself too
close to the ball and sliced down
to the inside to make the return.

FIG. 5–7 a, b, c
Return of serve—Rosewall's open stance,
high backhand return, contacted solidly in
front of the body in good balance.

**FIG. 5–8, a, b, c, d, e
Loyo-Mayo return of serve**—the
follow-through on this closed
stance return of serve indicates
an offensive shot hit cross-court.

FIG. 5–9, a, b, c
Return of serve—Sullivan
attacking a serve inside
the baseline with a level,
short swing.

Against fast serves you are working at the limits of human capability in reaction time and adjustment to various bounces. Standing in one spot, a fast-reacting tennis player requires 0.37 seconds to play a ball. (This time factor was obtained by studying motion pictures and measuring the volley exchange time required for a good return off another volley. If the time from the moment the ball was on the opponent's racket until it was in a position of contact, without the necessity of moving the feet, was less than 0.37 seconds, the ball was unplayable; that is, the time was not adequate for human reaction.) If a receiver must move two steps to get his racket on a hard, first serve, the serve will be an ace, because the time is too short for both reaction and movement. Thus, if the service court were narrowed by one foot, the contest between server and receiver would be more equal.

chapter 6

THE SMASH AND LOB

There are certain important differences between hitting a smash and hitting a serve. Because in a smash you do not have control of the ball as when serving, you are generally moving backward to position yourself under the lob. This forces variations in footwork and generally a difference in racket preparation before swinging. To move backward, the right foot must be dropped back immediately, to enable either a side skipping or a turn and run. You try to end up standing sideways as in serving, but more than likely you will be jumping off the right foot and landing on the left (off the left onto the right for the left-hander, as in Figure 6–1). The backswing is more of a pickup to the side and behind the head preparing for the smash, rather than the long, circular backswing of the serve. If you are not agile enough for this jumping swing, play slightly deeper in the court against a good lobber. No matter how you move, you are trying to strike the ball out in front of you at optimum height and off the right shoulder. It can be struck further forward than a serve because you are standing closer to the net and have the whole court to use. This eliminates the need for spin, so that the ball can be hit flat (meaning that the racket face is perpendicular and the racket swing is in line with the ball flight). Although you are striving to get set so

**FIG. 6–1 a, b, c, d
Smash**—the jump backwards and the change from the left to the right foot during a smash to free the left foot for the stretch at impact (left hander).

that the adjustment of body weight to the front foot can be executed, you probably won't be able to. If the ball gets past you, you must not only jump and hit, but make special adjustments with the arm and hand to get the racket behind the ball properly (Figure 6–2). A hard smash that is put away consistently is certainly the mark of a good athlete. An overhead that is placed consistently is the mark of a practiced player. Getting into the proper court position remains the most difficult aspect of hitting overheads.

FIG. 6–2 a, b, c, d
Smash—after stopping for the smash, the player had to make additional body adjustments to get the racket on the ball properly. The weight stayed on the left foot to allow the right foot pickup.

Not very much can be written about the lob, and yet its effective use can annihilate an opponent. The touch, deception, and choice of when to use it can be practiced only during play. The basic stroke is an upward swing in the direction of ball flight with a shortened backswing, with the racket face perpendicular to ball flight. This would also make it more permissible to drop the racket head prior to impact without fear of error. It is not a ground stroke hit with underspin, but a flat, slow-moving racket following the ball. The shortened backswing is needed simply because the ball is hit softly. Slight variations in racket face angle are dependent upon the ball's bounce and flight before impact. The heavy topspin lob is a specialty that requires great accuracy, and it should be attempted only occasionally, if at all.

chapter 7

EQUIPMENT DESIGN

SELECTING A RACKET

Size and weight markings are not adequate for the proper selection of a racket. The racket handle size and overall weight do not always agree with the markings of the manufacturer. The grip size, overall weight, center of gravity, flexibility, and the string and its tension are all important variables.

The grip size varies with hand size, and one indicator of proper size is the placement of the tip of the thumb in a forehand grip. With the fingers properly spread, the tip of the thumb should fall just beyond the first knuckle of the second finger. If it just reaches the first knuckle, the grip is probably too large, and if it falls close to the second knuckle, it is probably too small.

I believe that most players should use a racket head that is not too heavy: a strung racket that weighs 350 to 370 grams for women, and 370 to 395 grams for men (12.3 to 13 ounces and 13 to 13.9 ounces, respectively). These weights will make it easier to acquire a controlled swing as well as help prevent sore arms. A heavier racket should help one to hit a faster ball, but accuracy and consistency remain the main problems of most tennis players. As explained in the serve, grip firmness is just as important as racket weight in ball speed. A critical appraisal of results ob-

tained is equally important for tournament players when select-
ing racket weights. Appendix B presents additional data on ball
velocities and striking mass. When a person speaks of a player
hitting a "heavy ball," he means that the ball velocity was greater
than anticipated from the racket swing speed. The term is simply
a compliment on a player's grip firmness at impact.

The racket's center of gravity is important because it has more
effect on the "feel" of the racket weight than does total weight.
A light racket that is head heavy may feel too heavy, whereas a
heavier racket with the balance point nearer the handle may feel
light. If the balance point is beyond 13 1/2" from the end of the
handle, the racket will feel heavy. The balance point also affects
the center of percussion. If a ball hits the strings at the center of
percussion, the force transmitted to the base of the index finger
will be minimal. Racket designers make most rackets so that the
center of percussion is in the middle of the strings if the racket
is held with the butt end just outside the hand. If the hand position is changed on the grip, the center of percussion is also
changed, because the pivotal point during impact is also changed.
The racket tends to rotate out of the hand during impact, revolving about the base of the index finger while the rest of the fingers
close tightly to counter this torque. Swing tips raise the center
of percussion toward the head, but also make it difficult to maintain desired balance. If you are particular about equipment, you
should know where the center of gravity and center of percussion
are for your racket according to your grip (Appendix C).

Frame flexibility is easily measured if you hang a weight at
the tip while the handle is solidly clamped. The tip displacement
is then measured using various weights. Measurements for many
well-known rackets are presented in Appendix D. The greater
the flexibility, the less the force of impact, and the less force
transmitted to the hand. This increase in the time of impact lessens
the speed of the ball but makes it easier to hold the racket firmly,
in turn increasing ball velocity. These opposing results are com-
pensated with varying affects according to the racket velocity.
Given these facts about racket flexibility, a racket of medium
flex is probably most suitable for the majority of tennis players.
A tournament player may tend to use a stiff frame in the hope of
obtaining more ball speed, but the compensating factors men-
tioned can produce balls of equal speed with either a stiff or
flexible racket. The weekend player may be much more inter-
ested in preserving his arm and playing with accuracy, so a flex-

ible frame would be a wise choice. The hard hitter using a flexible frame must be aware of one other problem. The shaft bends a great deal owing to the ball's force of impact, and vibration after impact is great. The rebound of the shaft has been known to result in a sore arm as readily as the force of impact on a stiff frame (Figure 7–1).

FIG. 7–1
Selected frames at ball impact
taken at 4000 frames per second.

a. The ball has just touched the strings.

b. The ball is flattening against the strings.

c. The strings are pushed out the back side. The ball was hit slightly higher than the center, but the greatest depression is at the center, thus producing an elongated flattening.

d. The point of greatest ball flattening. Identical pictures of a non-pressure ball showed that the ball flattened to such an extent that it was completely hidden by the wooden frame. The coefficient of restitution of a non-pressure ball is less at high velocities, which means that a hard-hit ball will not travel as fast as a pressurized ball.

e. The racket is bent backward as the ball leaves the strings, and racket head vibrations of diminishing magnitudes begin.

f. The head is bending forward owing to the oscillation created by impact.

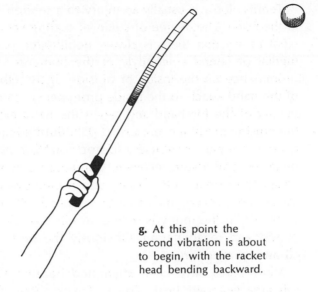

g. At this point the second vibration is about to begin, with the racket head bending backward.

The type of string and the tension are additional factors affecting ball control and speed. The tension varies with the size of the racket head as well as the setting of the stringing machine. It would be better to classify stringings by a musical note than by pounds. A small racket head requires less stringing tension to obtain the same amount of string deflection at impact as a larger head strung more tightly. A small head should have about four pounds less machine tension to get equal absolute tension, and most nylon strings should be about two pounds less than gut owing to the variance of resilient qualities. The most suitable tension is dependent upon the player's level of ability. My choices for gut strung rackets with a full head size based on my knowledge of equipment and players would be: 56 to 58 pounds for the occasional player, 58 to 62 pounds for the regular player. These figures are reduced by 2, 4, or 6 pounds if nylon, a small head, or both, respectively, are used. It must not be concluded that the only good stringing is a tight one.

TENNIS ELBOW: CAUSES AND TREATMENT

Injury to the elbow can result from improper body positions or improper use of the body, causing undue strain at the joint. The force due to ball impact is partially transmitted to the joint through the racket and the muscles and this, too, is a cause of tennis elbow.

Tennis elbow is usually an injury to a tendon or its attachment at the bone. The degree of strain or tearing varies, but it is sufficient to say that there is always debilitating pain on either the medial or lateral epicondyle of the humerus (the largest bony prominence on the inside or outside of the elbow). The flexors of the hand attach to the inside prominence, causing pain during impact of the forehand and serve; the hand extensors attach to the outside prominence, causing pain during impact of the backhand. Once pain is sufficient to stop you from playing, only complete rest will assure recovery. Continued play will probably increase the extent of the injury and prolong healing time. If the injury is not severe, play may be resumed within a week or two with care. If the injury is severe, it will take six to eight months of rest and rehabilitation. Obviously the best answer to tennis elbow is prevention.

Many cures have been attempted because tissue damage in this area generally heals slowly. Treatment is unreliable, and a period of no activity seems essential. The greatest mistake most people make is to continue play or go back to regular play before sufficient healing has taken place. After sufficient rest, a period of rehabilitation using light weights should be used for gradual strengthening of the arm. Arm curls with both palm up and palm down grip should exercise the forearm muscles involved (flexion and extension of the forearm). Start with 5 pounds in one hand and progress to 25 pounds before resuming controlled tennis practice.

The muscular contraction needed for even a moderate game of tennis is much greater during ball impact than most people realize. The muscular effort during a fast swing, with its resulting fast deceleration, also is much greater than one would expect. This effort results in sore shoulders, pulled muscles, and tennis elbow, because a player often exceeds the limit of his muscular fitness. Extra-long playing sessions, a change in racket, or an unexpected bounce may cause a muscle strain. The muscular fitness of an individual must be equal to the stresses of the game he plays or injuries such as tennis elbow are inevitable.

Because the choice of racket affects the force transmitted to the arm muscles at impact, anyone who has already had some problems should use a light racket, not head heavy, of medium flex and strung about 56 pounds with gut. Arm trouble often develops with a change in rackets. A heavier, stiffer, or more tightly strung racket will increase the muscle required during the swing and at impact, and only a slight difference may be enough to cause injury. The body is highly adaptable, but in a very specific manner. Specificity of fitness is characteristic of any sport. Change the pattern of demands on the body and some part may not be able to withstand the changes. The soundest advice for the average player is to choose equipment with care and hit everything with moderate speed.

APPENDIX

Appendix

Ball Flight

A serve hit at 150 feet per second (102 miles per hour) from 9' above the ground at an angle of 5° downward with no spin would pass 4.52' above the ground when passing over the net, and hit over 7' out of the court. This ball velocity, hitting height, and angle were chosen because they are close to what the actual first serve of a tall man is likely to be.

The spin placed on the ball causes most of the added drop necessary to put the ball in court. Air resistance and wind conditions are added factors.

If no margin of error were used over the net, the ball would hit just inside the service court with no spin. Only the tallest men hit the serve that high above the ground, a fact that points out even more the necessity for spin.

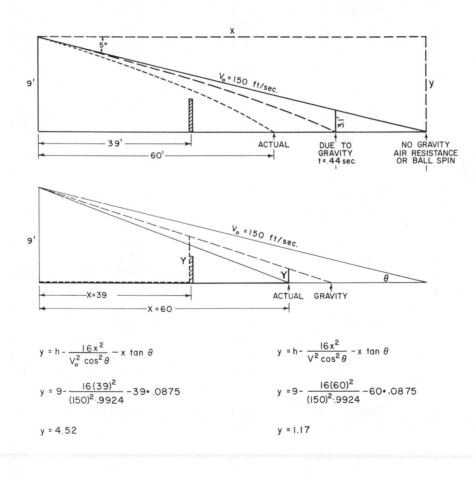

$$y = h - \frac{16x^2}{V_o^2 \cos^2\theta} - x \tan\theta$$

$$y = 9 - \frac{16(39)^2}{(150)^2 \cdot .9924} - 39 \cdot .0875$$

$$y = 4.52$$

$$y = h - \frac{16x^2}{V^2 \cos^2\theta} - x \tan\theta$$

$$y = 9 - \frac{16(60)^2}{(150)^2 \cdot .9924} - 60 \cdot .0875$$

$$y = 1.17$$

Striking Mass

The table shows the change in the striking mass of selected balls of various speeds.

RACKET	BALL VELOCITY AFTER IMPACT (mph)	RACKET VELOCITY BEFORE IMPACT (mph)	STRIKING MASS (grams)
Dunlop	60.0	66.5	203
Fort 4 1/2 L	69.0	75.5	226
	75.0	87.0	324
	85.0	95.0	202
	89.0	105.0	167
Bancroft			
Aussie 4 1/2 M	63.0	68.0	221
	72.0	72.5	381
	78.0	83.0	298
	85.5	87.0	281
	98.0	95.0	256
Bancroft	63.0	64.5	250
Executive 4 5/8 M	69.0	68.0	298
	76.0	77.5	248
	83.0	79.0	328
	89.5	102.0	172
Cragin S			
Prof. 4 5/8 M	63.0	67.0	250
	68.5	77.0	225
	74.0	77.0	319
	88.0	88.0	313
	98.0	107.0	246
Sirt	58.0	63.0	213
Nylon 4 1/2 L	68.5	71.0	310
	71.5	77.0	226
	90.0	91.0	275
	97.0	111.0	223
Wilson	62.0	63.5	293
Aluminum 4 5/8 M	72.0	78.0	314
	78.0	86.5	275
	87.0	86.5	318
	87.0	112.0	205

These data were measured from slow-motion pictures and the striking mass was calculated. The rackets vary in weight, flex, size, and strings. All are gut strung except the Sirt. The Aussie has a stiff frame, the Executive has a swing tip, placing the center of gravity closest to the impact point, and is also the heaviest. The Cragin-Simplex has a flexible wood frame to compare with the Wilson metal frame. The Italian Sirt is about the same weight as the Wilson and equally head weighted. Comparisons indicate that the racket head before impact travels slightly faster than the resulting ball velocity. The light-headed rackets can be made to attain slightly higher velocities, but they do not give faster ball velocity. The biggest variable still remains the firmness of the grip; it has much more influence on ball speeds than does selection of a racket. No single racket seems to be best for either hitting a ball faster or hitting with more consistent grip firmness.

APPENDIX C

Center of Percussion

Mark that point on the handle where the palm just below the index finger touches the handle. Suspend the racket from this point and swing it in a small arc, and measure the time of one full swing (over and back). This is done with a sweep second hand stop watch, measuring the time of 10 swings and dividing by 10. The center of percussion is then found, using the following formula:

$$qr = k^2 \quad k^2 = l/m \quad l = t^2 mgr/4\pi^2$$
$$qr = t^2 mgr/4\pi^2 m \quad q = t^2 g/4\pi^2$$

$$q = t^2\ 32.2 \times 12/\ 39.48 = \text{inches from pivot point}$$

q = distance from pivot point to center of percussion
l = moment of inertia of irregular shape
m = mass
g = gravity
r = distance from pivot point to center of gravity
k = radius of gyration

If the period (t) were found to be 1.3 seconds, the center of percussion would be 16.5" from the swing point. If this point were 4" from the end of the handle (as determined by your grip), the center of percussion would be 20.5" from the handle end. Most racket head centers are about 21.5" from the end, so this would indicate that the racket is not suited for you, or you should move your grip up slightly toward the head.

Racket Data

RACKET and SIZE	WEIGHT (grams)	CENTER OF GRAVITY (centimeters)	12 1/2 DEFLECTION (centimeters)
Dunlop Fort 4 1/2 L	358	34.3	2.4
Italian Sirt "	362	33.0	2.1
Sterling Metal "	386	33.0	3.3
Tensor Metal 4 3/8 L	365	33.2	2.4
Bancroft Aussie 4 1/2 M	376	33.8	2.1
Italian Sirt "	370	32.6	2.0
Australian Oliver (International)	388	34.5	2.6
Australian Oliver (Sedgeman)	396	34.0	2.5
Italian Royal Blue (Sedgeman)	375	34.0	2.2
Bancroft FRS Competition	390	32.8	2.2
Bancroft Executive 4 5/8	393	35.3	2.2
Cragin Simplex Professional	398	34.4	2.7
"	376	33.7	2.4
Wilson Aluminum	376	33.8	3.2
Spalding Gonzales	373	34.0	1.9
"	385	34.4	2.1
"	415	34.5	1.8
Wilson Kramer	383	34.0	1.9
Spalding Davis Cup	383	33.1	2.3
"	376	33.5	2.1
Bancroft FRS	393	34.8	2.3
Davis Supreme	398	34.3	2.5
Davis TAD	390	34.2	2.7
Australian Oliver (Sedgeman)	396	33.4	2.3
Wilson Aluminum 4 3/4 M	370	33.1	3.2

With the heads clamped solidly at top and bottom, a rebound test was done. Comparing rackets with string tensions of equal sound, rather than equal string tension, the small-headed rackets had a slightly greater rebound at equal ball speeds, and the Wilson Aluminum had the least rebound. However, the coefficient of restitution varied only from 0.82 to 0.87 for all rackets at a ball velocity of 30 to 33 miles per hour with the head clamped.

The table above indicates the differences between rackets with the same handle size and weight markings. It also shows the variations in balance and flex. Twelve and one-half pounds were hung on the racket tip with the handle clamped. Deflection for a stiff racket could be classified as from 1.8 to 2.2 centimeters, a medium flex as from 2.3 to 2.7 centimeters, and a very flexible racket, from 2.8 to 3.3 centimeters.

Any balance point 34 centimeters or over is beyond the 13.5" from the end of the handle, and will probably feel head heavy to most people. A racket weighing 400 grams or more should be classified as heavy, and probably avoided by most players. The table will help you to select the racket that will fulfill your needs. Don't be influenced by what tournament players use or by the many claims of advertising.

INDEX